Always Sisters

Always Sisters

Becoming the Princess
You Were Created to Be

Devotional and Guided Journal

HOWARD BOOKS
A DIVISION OF SIMON & SCHUSTER
New York   London   Toronto   Sydney

CeCe Winans
with Claudia Mair Burney

Our purpose at Howard Books is to:

• Increase faith in the hearts of growing Christians
• Inspire holiness in the lives of believers
• Instill hope in the hearts of struggling people everywhere
Because He's coming again!

HOWARD
BOOKS

Published by Howard Books, a division of Simon & Schuster, Inc.
1230 Avenue of the Americas, New York, NY 10020
www.howardpublishing.com
Always Sisters © 2007 by CeCe Winans

Library of Congress Cataloging-in-Publication Data

Winans, CeCe.
  Always sisters : becoming the princess you were created to be / CeCe Winans.
    p. cm.
  Summary: "Devotional book for teen girls"—Provided by publisher.
  1. Teenage girls—Religious life. 2. African American teenage girls—Religious life. 3. Teenage girls—Prayers and devotions.
  4. African American teenage girls—Prayers and devotions. 5. Self-esteem in adolescence—Religious aspects—Christianity. I. Title.
  II. Claudia Mair Burney.
  BV4860.W56 2007
  248.8'33—dc22

                                2007003985
  ISBN-13: 978-1-4165-4339-8
  ISBN-10: 1-4165-4339-2

10 9 8 7 6 5 4 3

HOWARD and colophon are registered trademarks of Simon & Schuster, Inc.

Manufactured in the United States

For information regarding special discounts for bulk purchases, please contact: Simon & Schuster Special Sales at 1-800-456-6798 or business@simonandschuster.com.

Edited by Philis Boultinghouse
Cover design by Terry Dugan Design
Interior design by Stephanie D. Walker
Photos on pages iii, 135, and 143 by Kwaku Alston Photography
Illustrations by GettyImages
"Always Sisters" © Priscilla Love, Angelique Lynette Winans, and Debra Renee Winans. All rights reserved. Used by permission.

Contents

CONTENTS

Acknowledgments

With any major project, it takes a great team to bring it all together. I want to thank those wonderful people who help me do all that I do, including the completion of this book.

To Tammy Bennett—thanks for introducing us to people who would care about the idea.

Chrys Howard and Philis Boultinghouse—without your expertise this project wouldn't have been possible. Thank you for believing in me and my ministry.

Claudia Mair Burney—thanks for putting the words from my heart on paper. I pray they will change the hearts of many.

Demetrus Stewart—thank you for your passion and love for the next generation. Your hard work and great efforts will cause a great harvest for the Kingdom.

Alvin Love—your love, support, and encouragement keep me going with a smile. I love you and thank you for all you do. I'm glad you are my husband.

Alvin and Ashley—thank you for being the blessings that you are. I pray that God's favor rest upon you.

To all my family—the Winans and the Loves, I thank you all for the important parts you play in my life.

Pastor Horace and Kiwanis Hockett—your covering keeps me under the shadow of the Almighty. Thanks for making it plain.

To Erma Byrd—thanks for letting the world know about this book and all God has assigned us to do.

—CeCe Winans

A chosen generation

You are a chosen generation,
a royal priesthood, a holy nation,
His own special people, that you
may proclaim the praises of Him
who called you out of darkness
into His marvelous light.

—*1 Peter 2:9 NKJV*

INTRODUCTION

I WAS BLESSED to have people, especially women of God, in my life who often reminded me of this scripture and the fact that I was chosen, that I was royalty, and that I could stand and proclaim God's praises in the world. Their constant teachings about how God viewed me and what He thought about me gave me the courage and the confidence to go through life expecting great things. I have known all my life that the favor of God was upon me, and that has made all the difference. It has shaped me into the woman I am today, and those teachings will continue to shape me into exactly what God wants me to be—the best!

God's Word is a *"lamp unto my feet, and a light unto my path"* (Psalm 119:105 KJV). When we allow God's Word to rule every area of our lives, it shines bright on every situation, conflict, and trial, and it gives us the insight we need to make the right decisions and choices through life. The sooner you start allowing God's Word to be your compass, the better you will be. I am a witness that God will *"never leave you nor forsake you"* (Deuteronomy 31:8 NIV). If you put Him first in your life, He really will make everything better than alright.

It is my desire that every young lady who reads this book will learn that she is a princess chosen by God to be in His royal family and that Jesus Christ is her Friend and King. God will supply all your needs according to His riches in glory through Christ Jesus (see Philippians 4:19). You are fearfully and wonderfully made (see Psalm 139:14), and you are so precious in God's sight. So stand strong, be of good courage (see Joshua 1:9), and know that no weapon formed against you shall prosper (see Isaiah 54:17). I don't care who you are, where you come from, or how sad you might feel. You are more than a conqueror, you are beautiful inside and out, and the Lord God Almighty has a very bright future in store for you because you are His princess now and forever! *"Delight yourself in the Lord and he will give you the desires of your heart"* (Psalm 37:4 NIV).

Yes, it's true all you have to do is fall in love with Jesus by spending time with Him, praying, reading, and obeying His Word, and God will give you your heart's desire. Take it from me, if you want to live a happy, fulfilled, successful life, Princess, love the Lord God your King and Father with all your heart, soul, mind, and body.

The Power of a Princess

The princess is in the palace—
How beautiful she is!

—*Psalm 45:13* TEV

You Are a Daughter of the King

THE MUSIC VIDEO shows a young man rapping verses over a throbbing beat. In the video, everything revolves around him. He sets himself up as a king, dripping with gold chains and diamond pendants shaped like his initials, rims, and even a cross. He's fully dressed, but the young women spinning around him have very little on. No matter. The scantily clad video girls are an accessory, no more valuable than the cheap chains around his neck. They are useful only as long as they please the rapper. When something bigger, shinier, or prettier comes along, he discards them.

Nobody knows the video girls' names. Nobody looks into their eyes. Their attention is focused on the parts of the girls' bodies that God meant to be secret. Do you think these girls feel special?

Once, you were just like those video girls. You were a slave to sin. But Jesus noticed you. He's far more powerful and much richer than a rap star. And He's definitely more compassionate. Jesus scooped you up in His gentle hands. He didn't

3

leave you to die. He picked you up from the muck and mire you were trapped in, looked into your eyes, and fell in love with you. He cleaned you up and told you to *live* (see Ezekiel 16:6–7). Then He did something truly amazing: He adopted you (see Ephesians 1:4–5).

You are part of a royal family. Galatians 3:26 says, *"For you are sons [and daughters] of God through faith in Christ Jesus"* (NASB). *"God has sent forth the Spirit of His Son into your hearts crying out, 'Abba, Father!'"* (Galatians 4:6 NASB). *Abba* is the privileged, deeply personal way to say *Father*. It's like calling God *Daddy*. You are the King's beloved baby, His priceless princess.

He also offers His tender father care, always: *"Do not worry about your life, what you will eat or what you will drink; nor about your body, what you will put on"* (Matthew 6:25 NKJV). Our great God, King of all Kings, promises to clothe you in a splendor that rivals the lilies of the field (see Matthew 6:28–29). Jesus said even King Solomon in all his glory was not arrayed as beautifully as those flowers. And you will be clothed in greater garments, Princess.

Wear your crown with joy! Your shining robe of righteousness. Walk in the light He's given you. You are rescued. You are saved. You are His, the daughter of the King.

SISTER TIP

If you see your sister slipping into the video-girl role, remind her that she is a member of a royal family and that Jesus the King is her rescuer, ready to save her and bring her into His royal family.

Journal Questions

1. Behind the glamour and the glitz of the video girls' outward appearance, what sorrows might be hiding?

_____

_____

_____

_____

_____

_____

_____

2. How does a princess behave?

_____

_____

_____

_____

_____

_____

3. How does knowing Jesus change how you feel about yourself?

_____

_____

_____

_____

_____

_____

4. Read Psalm 18:16–24. Write about a time you've gotten yourself into a real mess and longed for someone to rescue you, support you, and really love you.

_____

_____

_____

_____

_____

_____

5. You are always a princess, but your crown is invisible. How do you juggle your dual citizenship as a resident of God's Kingdom and the world at the same time?

_____

_____

_____

_____

_____

_____

_____

You are no longer foreigners
and aliens, but fellow citizens
with God's people
and members of God's household.
Ephesians 1:19 NIV

I will praise You

I will praise You, for I am fearfully and wonderfully made; Marvelous are Your works, and that my soul knows very well.

—*Psalm 139:14 NASB*

You Are Beautifully and Wonderfully Made

TAKE A LOOK in the mirror. What do see?

Are your flaws the first thing you see—or what you *think* are your flaws? Maybe you get discouraged sometimes because you don't look like a fashion model. Maybe you think your hips are too wide. Or that your lips are too thick or thin. Or your breasts too small or too large. Too many young women, even the ones who know they're God's princesses, neglect celebrating their unique beauty. This is a shame before God, who created you to be the crown jewel of Creation.

Sister, don't waste your time being down on yourself. Fashion models exist to sell clothes or products. They have a team of stylists and makeup artists to make them look good. And you'd be surprised at what can be done with tape and creative camera angles! Did you know that after the glamorous photo shoots, those perfect-looking models get their pictures touched up, air-brushed, and enhanced by the art department?

Don't you spend one minute comparing yourself to someone else. Who is like you? Nobody. Even if you found someone with your exact same name, she wouldn't be you.

God sees you as magnificent, just as you are. He worked out every tiny detail that makes you who you are—a beautiful young woman made in His own image. You are God's look-alike!

God knows the number of hairs on your head. He's counted every freckle and mole on the landscape of your body. He intimately drew each swirling line that makes up your fingerprints. Your lovely skin color is mixed from a palette all His own. You are an original, the only one of your kind. You're not flawed because God doesn't make mistakes. In God's eyes, you're *all that*. David, the psalmist knew this truth. He wrote: *"You created my inmost being; you knit me together in my mother's womb"* (Psalm 139:13 NIV).

But there is more, Princess. When you accepted Christ as your King and became His baby girl, God gave you even more gifts. In Christ you are:

- Forgiven of all your sins.
- Loved now and eternally.
- Cherished, as God's own child.
- Completely and utterly accepted.

Yes, Sister, you're all that.

Take a look in the mirror again. Do you see what God sees? Do you see the stunning beauty He created? The designer original? Tenderly crafted by His own hands?

God sees how amazing you are every single time.

Always Sisters
SISTER TIP

Be a positive mirror for your sister. When she puts herself down, be right there beside her to build her up. Tell her what is beautiful about her.

Journal Questions

1. Write down what you believe God thinks of you.

_____

_____

_____

_____

_____

_____

_____

_____

2. Is it difficult to see yourself as God sees you? If so, why?

_____

_____

_____

_____

_____

3. What are some tricks the Devil uses to convince princesses that they are not what God says they are?

_____

_____

_____

_____

_____

4. Psalm 139:13 says God knit you together in your mother's womb. What are some special qualities God knit into you?

_____

_____

_____

_____

_____

5. Write a prayer of praise to God, listing specific things about yourself that you are thankful for. Think of things you take for granted that you really would be miserable without.

_____

_____

_____

_____

_____

_____

The LORD will fulfill His purpose for me; your love, O LORD, endures forever—Do not abandon the works of your hands.

Psalm 138:8 NIV

I give unto you power

Behold I give unto you power to tread on serpents and scorpions; and over all the power of the enemy: and nothing shall by any means hurt you.

—Luke 10:19 KJV

Your Princess Power Comes from the King of Kings

As a PRINCESS you may not want to think about treading on serpents and scorpions. Stomping on creepy things makes a big mess or, worse, that yucky crunch sound. Ew! Doing good works, wearing lovely gowns to the King's feasts, and feeding the poor are much nicer than trampling icky creatures. But being in the Royal family, you *will* go to war. Everyone in the Kingdom is called to fight, including God's princesses. Matthew 11:12 says, *"And from the days of John the Baptist until now, the kingdom of heaven suffereth violence, and the violent take it by force"* (KJV). You can't be delicate during war. You must be a fierce warrior princess.

If you had to go to battle, where would your power come from? Would charm be your power? Would beauty be your weapon against evil? During war, you have to remember the wise words of Proverbs: *"Charm is deceptive, and beauty is fleeting; but a woman who fears the LORD is to be praised"* (Proverbs 31:30 NIV). The Word of God says, *"The thief only comes to steal, kill, and destroy"* (John 10:10 WEB). Dealing with your deadliest foe requires power from on high—the Jesus kind of power.

Jesus knows that sometimes you have to take off your tiara, roll up the sleeves of your gown, and wrestle with the enemy. He made a plan for you. Just before He was taken up to heaven (see Acts 1:2), Jesus commanded His chosen ones to *"wait for the promise of the Father"* (Acts 1:4 NKJV). He knows you can do nothing without His power, so He gave it, starting in a crowded prayer room, many years ago.

God poured out the Holy Spirit, just as Jesus promised: *"But you will receive power when the Holy Spirit comes on you; you will be my witnesses in Jerusalem, and in all Judea, and Samaria, and to the ends of the earth"* (Acts 1:8 NIV). God is still pouring out His Spirit, right now! It's for all of His children. It's for *you*, part of your birthright in the royal family of God.

Don't just walk in the *beauty* of being a new creation in Christ. Receive your power and walk in your *authority* to defeat the enemy in Jesus's name. You are designed for the Kingdom. You possess the power of the King of Kings. Hold your head high and claim the power of the King of Kings!

When the going gets tough, a sister stands firm. Being a princess isn't all rose gardens and tea parties. Sometimes a princess has to stand and fight—or, at the very least, hold her ground. That's when she needs you—her sister—to stand close beside her, always pointing her to the only real source of power, her heavenly King of Kings.

Journal Questions

1. All members of the Kingdom of God must go to war with the enemy of our souls: the Devil. Write about a time when you felt you were battling Satan.

_____

_____

_____

_____

_____

_____

_____

2. Do you think God wants you to be afraid of the Devil? What is a healthy attitude to take about spiritual warfare?

_____

_____

_____

_____

_____

_____

3. Read 1 Peter 5:8 NIV. God's Word describes the Devil as a killer *lion*. Write down some ways the Devil roars and prowls around in your personal life.

_____

_____

_____

_____

_____

4. Now write some ways the Holy Spirit overcomes the enemy with His power.

_____

_____

_____

_____

_____

5. Name some occasions where you should have taken a stand but didn't. Write a prayer to God, and ask Him for strength and gentleness and courage to face the next challenge in a way that would please God.

_____

_____

_____

_____

_____

_____

I pray also that the eyes of your heart may be enlightened in order that you may know the hope to which He has called you, the riches of His glorious inheritance in the saints.

Ephesians 2:18 NIV

I'm not asking that you take them
out of the world
But that you guard them
from the Evil One.

—John 17:15 MSG

Princesses Are Trained Not To Fit In

LONG BEFORE YOU were a sparkle in your mother's eyes, Jesus knew you. He knew that you are unique—one of a kind—and that you are purposed for amazingly wonderful things. And He knew from the start that as a princess, you would be trained *not* to fit in.

Jesus also knows all about this world, and He knows that it can be a treacherous place. And so He put you on His personal prayer list: "I'm not asking that you take them out of the world, but that you guard them from the Evil One" (John 17:15 MSG). When Jesus prayed this prayer, He knew the terrible fate of the cross that awaited Him. The moment Jesus said, "It is finished," and died on the cross is the most magnificent moment that ever was or will be. Although it was a magnificent moment for humankind, the cross was a horrific experience for the man Jesus. Yet Jesus did not shrink from the horror of it, for He fully understood that in order for you to live, He must die. So when He prayed for you, He did it knowing full well the sacrifice He must make on your behalf. And, Princess, He did it because He believed you were worth it.

Jesus knew you are from a Kingdom that is not of this world. You are different, Princess, for you have a heavenly crown. The children of the world cannot see your crown, but they can see that you are not like them. You speak the truth in love. You walk as if you are led by the Spirit. You don't lie or cheat. You respect yourself and others. You are a young woman of grace—God's unmerited, undeserved favor.

In the kingdoms of this world, princesses are not common folk. They reside in a different, higher class. If you took a princess's royal robes and crown and placed her in plain garments in a room full of young ladies dressed much nicer, she would still stand out. Princesses are not normal or ordinary. They are like their Father: trained *not* to fit in.

The book of Romans offers encouragement for how to live. *"Therefore I urge you brothers [and sisters], in view of God's mercy, to offer your bodies as living sacrifices, holy and pleasing to God—this is your spiritual act of worship. Do not be conformed any longer to the pattern of this world, but be transformed by the renewing of your mind. Then you will be able to test and approve what God's will is—his good, pleasing, and perfect will"* (Romans 12:1–2 NIV).

All the answers are right there in the Word of God. Offer yourself—your body and soul—to God. It's as simple as saying, "Jesus, I am yours," and acting as if that is true. Read your Bible to train your mind to think more like Him. That will equip you, Princess, to know what God's will is. No matter where you are and no matter what the world says you should be, you will walk confidently, as He wants you to.

You belong to God.

When everyone else is pulling on your sister, trying to make her conform, be sure that your voice is the one that calls her higher, that helps her remember who she is and what she stands for. Look up, Sister, and lift your sister's chin to follow your gaze.

Journal Questions

1. How are you different from the world?

_____

_____

_____

_____

_____

_____

_____

_____

2. In what ways could you be more like Christ?

_____

_____

_____

_____

_____

_____

3. What difference does spending time in God's Word make in your daily life as a Christian?

_____

_____

_____

_____

_____

_____

4. Read John 17. What did Jesus pray that God would do for you?

_____

_____

_____

_____

_____

_____

5. Write a prayer of praise, thanking God for making you a princess who is worthy of every good thing He has planned for you. Ask Him to remind you when you should be different and not try to fit in.

_____

_____

_____

_____

_____

_____

Do your best to improve your faith. You can do this by adding goodness, understanding, self-control, patience, devotion to God, concern for others, and love. If you keep growing this way, it will show that what you know about our Lord Jesus Christ has made your lives useful and meaningful.

2 Peter 1:5–8 CEV

Pray without ceasing

Pray without ceasing.

—*I Thessalonians 5:17 KJV*

Your Power Source: Big Prayer... Big Power

FIRST THESSALONIANS 5:17 is a little scripture, but it packs a big punch, doesn't it? It shows how much *everyone* needs prayer, and lots of it!

Good things come from spending time talking to God. You get to know Him better, and He gets to know you too, as a person willing to surrender her time and make the effort to be with Him. You can tell God your secrets. In prayer, you're free to ask God anything, in your own words.

Read the Lord's Prayer from the Bible paraphrase *The Message* (Matthew 6:7–13):

Our Father in heaven,

Reveal who you are.

Set the world right;

Do what's best—as above, so below.

Keep us alive with three square meals.

Keep us forgiven with you and forgiving others.

Keep us safe from ourselves and the Devil.

You're in charge!

You can do anything you want!

You're ablaze in beauty!

Yes. Yes. Yes.

Doesn't that make you want to pour out your heart to God, especially the part that says: Yes! Yes! Yes! You don't need to speak to your heavenly Father using words you heard in church but don't really understand. Prayer is about being God's friend. It's spending time talking with Him just as you'd talk to your best friend or anyone you love deeply.

Not only does prayer allow you to talk to God, but it opens the door for Him to answer you. And if you want to hear His words to you, you must keep your heart and mind open to His leading. He may speak to you through a sermon or a Bible study message or even a conversation with a friend. Prayer opens the door to two-way conversation.

Make prayer a grand adventure, Princess. The Holy Spirit, your power source, meets you in your secret prayer place. Big prayer is not about trying to impress God; it's about staying on your knees until you are more like Jesus—in thought, word, and deed. Big prayer yields big power—more time with the Holy Ghost, more power to do God's will. And little prayer—pitiful amounts of time with God—means you get little power. No prayer? Well . . . that means no power.

So pray without ceasing. You'll become a holy stick of dynamite!

Go there, with God.

Be the one to say, "Want me to say a quick prayer?" You don't have to act all high and holy; you just need to be real. Chances are, she'll be glad you asked; and fact is, God will be present when you join your hearts to talk to Him. Just try it.

Journal Questions

1. Take any Bible translation you have, and write the Lord's Prayer (Matthew 6:9–15) in your own words.

_____

_____

_____

_____

_____

_____

_____

2. Look at the words of Jesus (sometimes they're in red letters) in the Gospels. What kinds of things did Jesus pray for?

_____

_____

_____

_____

_____

_____

3. Read James 1:5–8 and 5:13–16. From this scripture, what can we learn about how we should pray?

_____

_____

_____

_____

_____

_____

4. What good things happen when you spend lots of time with God in prayer?

_____

_____

_____

_____

_____

5. Read Psalm 37:4. Write down some of the desires of your heart. Write a prayer asking God to guide you in shaping your desires to please Him.

_____

_____

_____

_____

_____

_____

_____

_____

The earnest prayer of a righteous person has great power and produces wonderful results.

James 5:16 NLT

LiViNG iN THE KiNGDoM

Set your mind on things above,
not on things on the earth.

—*Colossians 3:2 NKJV*

What's Up with Your Thought Life?

WHAT IF YOUR mind were like a blank canvas—white and full of possibilities? Now imagine if you possessed the skill of a fine artist and had a rich and varied palette of gorgeous colors: royal blues, shining yellows, vivid reds, lively greens, glowing oranges, and regal purples. You are free to paint flowers, sunsets, lovely faces—whatever you want. But what if you dipped your paint brush in a circle of black pigment and slashed the pristine canvas with crude, horrible words and images?

It wouldn't be pretty, would it?

When you came to Christ, ugliness filled every surface of the canvas of your mind. But Christ gave you a brand new canvas—a fresh start for a new thought life. *"If any man be in Christ, he is a new creature: old things are passed away; behold, all things are become new"* (2 Corinthians 5:17 KJV). God's Word is your palette, and in it you'll find all you need to create a beautiful new mind.

The scripture is clear: *"Finally [sisters] whatever is true, whatever is noble, whatever is right, whatever is pure, whatever is lovely, whatever is admirable—if anything is excellent or praiseworthy—think about such things"* (Philippians 4:8 NIV).

What's up with your thought life, Princess? Are you thinking about what is true, or are you filling your mind with the latest gossip, even if it's coming from a tabloid magazine in the checkout aisle at the grocery store? Do you cram your lovely crowned head with soap operas or movies that would make the angels of heaven avert their eyes? What about the music you listen to? Does it draw you closer to God or to the world?

Always remember you are God's princess. You belong to a Kingdom that is not of this world. Jesus said, *"Out of the overflow of the heart the mouth speaks"* (Matthew 12:34 NIV). If you were measured by your thoughts, how exactly would you measure up? Are you a princess, with your mind set on things above, in the Kingdom? Or are you a commoner, with your mind set on things of little value?

"We demolish arguments and every pretension that sets itself up against the knowledge of God, and we take captive every thought to make it obedient to Christ" (2 Corinthians 10:5 NIV). You are a powerful young woman! You have the power to *choose* the thoughts you dwell on. Impure thoughts may come into your head—even Jesus was tempted by Satan to think wrong thoughts—but you can take those thoughts captive (as the verse above says), just like Jesus did. You do this by using God's Word and by choosing to think on the kinds of things listed in Philippians 4:8.

It's your mind, Princess; take control. Keep your head in the sky!

Always SISTERS SISTER TIP

You can tell a lot about what's going on in your sister's head by the words that come out of her mouth. As her sister and her friend, your privilege and responsibility is to be a check for her thought life as she is a check for yours. Be loving, not preachy; be kind, not judgmental. Lift her thoughts to things above.

Journal Questions

1. What do you think Jesus meant when he said, *"Out of the overflow of the heart the mouth speaks"* (Matthew 12:34 NIV)?

_____

_____

_____

_____

_____

_____

2. How do your thoughts affect your actions?

_____

_____

_____

_____

_____

_____

3. The Bible says we should think on whatever is true, noble, right, and pure (see Philippians 4:8). Name some practical ways to direct your thoughts toward these things.

_____

_____

_____

_____

_____

_____

4. What are the consequences of not taking impure thoughts captive?

_____

_____

_____

_____

_____

_____

5. How do you think you can make a thought obey Christ?

_____

_____

_____

_____

_____

_____

_____

_____

May the words of my mouth and
the mediation of my heart be
pleasing in your sight, O Lord,
my rock and my redeemer.
Psalm 19:14 NIV

How can a young [woman]
keep [her] way pure?
By living according to your word.

—*Psalm 119:9 NIV*

GET THE WORD IN YOU

DID YOU KNOW that in the ancient church, believers memorized the psalms? All 150 of them! Sounds like a lot, doesn't it? But they didn't sit down and try to commit the words to memory the way you would cram for a test. People chanted or sang them like songs. It was a great way to get the Word in you.

How many songs do you know? Perhaps dozens that you sing in church right now. What about the songs on your iPod or MP3 player? They add up fast.

Think of the benefits of knowing the psalms like that. Imagine if you had all kinds of scripture committed to memory. What a wellspring you'd have to draw from when your soul feels as hot and parched as a desert.

The very first psalm (Psalm 1:1–3) makes a case for having the Word in you. Check it out from *The Message*:

> *How well God must like you—*
> *   you don't hang out at Sin Saloon,*

you don't slink along Dead-End Road,

 you don't go to Smart-Mouth College.

Instead you thrill to GOD's Word,

 you chew on Scripture day and night.

You're a tree replanted in Eden,

 bearing fresh fruit every month,

Never dropping a leaf,

 always in blossom.

Imagine yourself as a beautiful, flourishing tree in God's garden, with your limbs stretched toward heaven, lovely with glossy, green leaves. Then imagine that you blossom with sweet-smelling flowers in the springtime and later bear delicious fruit for harvest. You can grow just like this tree if you'll pour the Word of God into yourself. Look at the benefits of knowing God in 2 Peter 1:2–3: "*Grace and peace be yours in abundance through the knowledge of God and of Jesus our Lord. His divine power has given us everything we need for life and godliness through our knowledge of him*" (NIV).

You've got *grace* and *peace* and *everything* you need! That should make you pull out your Bible right now if you haven't already.

Verse 4 promises even more! "*He has given us his very great and precious promises, so that through them you may participate in the divine nature*" (NIV). God allows you, Princess, to participate in His divine nature. It can't get any better than that. Go ahead, run to God's promises, and through them participate in the very life of God and in His nature. It's where you belong.

 Always **Sisters** SISTER TIP

You could do it together—your sister and you: set a goal for daily Bible reading, and then talk about what you've read. You'll be absolutely amazed at what you'll discover about yourself, your sister, and your God.

Journal Questions

1. Why do you think the Scriptures emphasize that we should have the Word inside us?

_____

_____

_____

_____

_____

_____

_____

2. What are some practical ways you can memorize God's Word?

_____

_____

_____

_____

_____

_____

3. What benefit would praying the Scriptures have?

_____

_____

_____

_____

_____

_____

4. Read Psalm 119:11. How can putting God's Word in your heart keep you from
   sinning?

_____

_____

_____

_____

_____

_____

5. This book, *Always Sisters,* is about knowing who we are in Christ and supporting one another. How do you think you could share the experience of putting the Word inside you with another sister in Christ?

_____

_____

_____

_____

_____

_____

_____

Your word is a lamp to guide my
feet and a light for my path.
Psalm 119:105 NLT

Beat it, Satan!

Jesus' refusal was curt;
beat it, Satan!

—Matthew 4:10 MSG

Take the Devil Down!

When it came to dealing with the Devil, Jesus didn't play. Check out Matthew 4:1–11 (MSG). *"Shortly after Jesus was baptized, the Holy Spirit led Him into the wilderness. The devil came to Him, just as he comes to all of us. He told Jesus, 'Since you are God's Son, speak the word that will turn these stones into loaves of bread'"* (verse 3).

Jesus had fasted forty days. He was hungry. Notice the Devil's tactics and the spiritual warfare lessons we can learn from them: the Devil knew Jesus was God's Son and had the power to speak the word to make things happen, but Jesus used those words to take the Devil down.

Spiritual warfare lesson one: *The Devil knows who you are and what you can do.* Notice that Jesus responded with the weapon of God's Word: *"It takes more than bread to stay alive. It takes a steady stream of words from God's mouth"* (verse 4).

Lesson two: *Know more Word than the Devil*! How? By a steady stream of words from God's mouth going into your heart and mind.

When the Devil took Jesus to the Holy City, he said, *"Since you are God's Son, jump"* (verse 6). The Devil knows you, Princess. He can quote Scripture, in this case, Psalm 91: *"He has placed you in the care of angels. They will catch you so you won't so much as stub your toe on the stone"* (verse 6).

Lesson three: *The Devil will tempt you to do foolish things.* Know the Word—understand it. Jesus again answered with God's Word: *"Don't you dare test the Lord your God"* (verse 7).

And when the Devil finally showed Jesus all the glorious kingdoms of the earth and said He could have them if only He would bow and worship him, Jesus didn't bother to be polite. *"Beat it, Satan!"* He followed with the Word: *"Worship the Lord your God, and only him. Serve him with absolute single-heartedness"* (verses 10–11).

The Devil got out of there fast. Angels showed up with everything Jesus needed.

Lesson four: *Take the Devil down.* You can't be delicate with the enemy of your soul. You have to do battle with him. And it's a *spiritual* battle: *"The weapons we fight with are not weapons of the world. On the contrary, they have divine power to demolish strongholds"* (2 Corinthians 10:4 NIV).

We all get tempted, but Christ showed us how to prevail against our enemy. We must cast down any thought, action, or spirit that exalts itself against the knowledge of God. We can't have the knowledge of God unless we are steeped in His Word. The weapon is in the Word. Put the Word in your mouth like Jesus did.

You'll beat the Devil every time.

Always Sisters SISTER TIP

Sometimes a sister needs help in her battle against the Devil. That's where you come in. If you see your sister stumble or fall, don't stand over her, looking down on her; stoop down and help her up. Remember the scripture that says, "Two are better than one, because they have a good return for their work: If one falls down, his friend can help him up!" (Ecclesiastes 4:9–10 NIV). Take that, you devil!

Journal Questions

1. Why did the Devil use Scripture to tempt Jesus?

_____

_____

_____

_____

_____

_____

_____

_____

2. Jesus had fasted, so the Devil tempted him with food. Name some things you may be doing to follow God and a way the Devil can tempt you away from your spiritual goals.

_____

_____

_____

_____

_____

3. How did Jesus fight against the tricks of the enemy?

_____

_____

_____

_____

_____

_____

4. Write out some of your favorite scriptures that are useful for taking the Devil down (not just the scripture reference, but the whole scripture!).

_____

_____

_____

_____

_____

_____

5. List some ways you can pick up a sister who has fallen for one of the Devil's tricks. (Be sure and think of ways you'd like to be treated.)

_____

_____

_____

_____

_____

_____

_____

_____

"You are from God, little children, and have overcome them; because greater is He who is in you than he who is in the world."

1 John 4:4 NASB

The world is full of so-called prayer warriors who are prayer-ignorant. They're full of formulas and programs and advice, peddling techniques for getting what you want from God. Don't fall for that nonsense. This is your Father you are dealing with, and he knows better than you what you need. With a God like this loving you, you can pray very simply.

—*Matthew 6:7–8 MSG*

A Princess Can Ask Her Daddy for Anything!

EACH OF US has a father, but some fathers are better than others. Some fathers stay with mothers, and they raise healthy, happy children together. Other fathers die much too soon and leave their families bereft in a sea of grief. Then there are fathers who abuse alcohol and drugs and fathers who abuse their sweet little girls.

For some princesses, *father* is a good word. It reminds them of the first man who truly loved them. To them, he's part hero and part champion. He is the first person to give her a glimpse of the nature of God—a generous provider and loving protector.

But what if a princess didn't have such a good father? What if she didn't even know she was a princess until God finally found her after years of pain put on her by people who should have loved her? Maybe He found her huddled in a big mess of her own or someone else's making, filth and debris clinging to her clothes. But then God washed her clean and loved her. He made her part of His family. He became her very own, real-live Father. Still, she may need to be convinced. She's been disappointed so many times. To her, the word *father* is just letters strung together without meaning.

A lot of sisters feel like that. They have no concept of God as a loving Father because they have no idea what a loving father is. You can't learn the fatherhood of God by watching daddies on situation comedies or by making up your own version. But you can check out what the Bible says about God your Father: *"He [God] Himself has said, I will not in any way fail you nor give you up nor leave you without support. [I will] not, [I will] not in any degree leave you helpless nor forsake nor let [you] down (relax My hold on you)! [Assuredly not!]"* (Hebrews 13:5 AMP).

Even the best of earthly fathers can fail, give up, and die. But God is not an earthly father. No, your Father is King and God. He is omnipotent, which means all powerful. He is omnipresent—always there for you. You may not get the answer to your prayer that you thought you'd get, and your help may not come when you want it to. But God is never too late. You just have to trust Him.

You are truly a highly favored young woman of God. You can ask your Father *anything*. He will hear you! He will never forsake you. He will not let you down.

He loves you.

Always.

Always Sisters SISTER TIP

If your sister is a little shy about approaching the throne of the Almighty God, maybe you can hold her hand and take her there; help her get over the jitters we all feel in the presence of royalty. Whisper in her ear that she is a princess, a daughter of the King, and He is eager to hear her request and give her the desires of her heart. Visit His throne room together—make it a sister affair.

Journal Questions

1. Why do you think it's difficult for girls who did not have good father figures to trust God?

_____

_____

_____

_____

_____

_____

_____

2. Does the fact that God loves you mean you can be a spiritual brat and demand whatever you want whenever you want it? Would God be pleased with that kind of behavior?

_____

_____

_____

_____

_____

3. James 4:1–3 gives us some guidelines concerning our motives when we pray. With this in mind, list some things you might ask your Daddy for.

_____

_____

_____

_____

_____

_____

4. From what you know of God in Scriptures, describe Him as Father. List the Father characteristics He displays.

_____

_____

_____

_____

_____

5. Write down some occasions that would be good opportunities to pray with your sisters. Ask God for courage to approach them with the suggestion to pray and for their hearts to be open to the idea.

_____

_____

_____

_____

_____

_____

The Lord is like a father to his children, tender and compassionate to those who fear him.
Psalm 103:13 NLT

No weapon formed against
you shall prosper.

—Isaiah 54:17 NKJV

God's Got Your Back

SOMETIMES LIFE IS scary. Watch the news any given day, and you'll see that bad things happen even to good people. But it's not just violence that concerns a young woman of God. The daily cares of this world conspire to bring you down. You may wonder if you'll get good grades in school. Or if you'll get into the college of your choice? Will your hair grow!? And what in the world will you *wear*!? God cares about everything, big and small, that concerns you.

Jesus knew the world could be a perilous place. He walked this earth not just as God, but as a human being. He knows you will worry sometimes, and He offers you His kindness. Jesus said, *"Therefore I tell you, don't worry about your life, what you will eat or drink; or about your body, what you will wear. Is not life more important than food, and the body more than clothes? Look at the birds of the air; they do not sow or reap or gather into barns, and yet your heavenly Father feeds them. Are you not much more valuable than they?"* (Matthew 6:25–26 NIV).

And Jesus had to be thinking of young women when He said, *"So why do you worry about clothing? Consider the lilies of the field, how they grow; they neither toil nor spin; and yet I say to you that even Solomon in all His glory was not arrayed like one of these. Now if God so clothes the grass of the field, which today is, and tomorrow is thrown in the oven, will He not much more clothe you, O you of little faith?"* (Matthew 6:28-30 NKJV).

God dressed up a field of grass with lilies. And even though He knew the field would be plowed and burned, He made the grass and took care of it. He will do the same for you, Princess, and much more, because He loves you.

It is God's good pleasure to protect you. Just as a loving dad wouldn't hesitate to put food on the table to feed his babies, your God, your Father, will make haste to help you, provide for you, and be your sword and shield against life's dangers.

Remember what David, once a shepherd and later a king, said: *"The Lord is my Shepherd, I shall not be in want"* (Psalm 23:1 NIV).

You will never be left vulnerable, and remember, Princess, God's got your back.

When you see your sister looking over her shoulder, acting worried and preoccupied, don't get all upset and think she's ignoring you. It may be that she's allowing fear to creep in and take over. That's your cue to come along beside her and remind her that God's got her back, that He cares about her with everything in Him. And remember, Sister, He's got your back too.

Journal Questions

1. Jesus said, *"O you of little faith"* (Matthew 6:30 NKJV), when he talked to his followers about God's provision. Why do you think He said that?

_____

_____

_____

_____

_____

_____

2. Jesus said that to God you are much more valuable than the birds He feeds and the lilies He clothes. What are your thoughts about His care for you?

_____

_____

_____

_____

_____

_____

3. Write about a time when God provided for you, even when you couldn't see how He would do it.

_____

_____

_____

_____

_____

_____

4. Read Isaiah 43:2. Write about some deep waters or some fire you have traveled through. How did God make His help available to you?

_____

_____

_____

_____

5. Look up these scriptures on *fear* and see what word keeps showing up as the cure: Psalm 112:7; Proverbs 29:25; and Psalm 56:3–4, 11. *Hint*: It starts with "t."

_____

_____

_____

_____

_____

_____

God is our refuge and
strength, an ever-present
help in trouble.
Psalm 46:1 NIV

Dealing with a Prince

You are the light

You are the light of the world.
A city on a hill cannot be hidden.

—*Matthew 5:14 NIV*

Shine Your Light On

Imagine walking into a dark room. In the pitch-black, you may as well be blind. Instinctively you hold your hands out in front of you. Maybe you inch forward, but something catches your knee, nearly toppling you over. You scramble away, only to stumble into something else. Finally you stop, hoping for just a sliver of light to help guide you through.

It doesn't take much light to dispel the darkness. Night-lights may not be good to read by, but they allow you to see enough to get through a room without hurting yourself. If you turn on a lamp, you can see even better than with the night-light, and flipping the switch on the ceiling light will chase away *all* the darkness in the room.

What do you think a world without God would be like? Can you imagine the chaos? Hurt, confusion, and sin would run rampant. People would drown in despair because life would hold no meaning. No one would hope. Love wouldn't exist.

But when Jesus went to be with the Father God, He left the light on. And that light is *you*. Jesus left you as His representative in the world. But you are not alone. He also sent the Holy Spirit to dwell *inside* you. Princess, you are the light of the world—the night-light, lamp, or ceiling light for everyone around you. Your life can keep others from stumbling in the dark.

Jesus likened you to a city high on a hill. A city on a hill can be seen even from a distance. You can't be hidden, and this is by God's design. Who else will reflect God to a world with no hope of knowing His love? *"Let your light shine before men, so that they may see your good deeds and praise your Father in heaven"* (Matthew 5:16 NIV).

A wise man once said that we should always preach the gospel, and sometimes we should use words. You are a walking Bible for those who have yet to discover God's Word. The things you do, how you treat others should all proclaim the Good News: God loves the world and will save us from the darkness of sin if we will only accept Him. Being the Good News doesn't mean you go around spouting scripture with no love or holiness behind your words; rather, it means that you live an acceptable life, pleasing to God.

Shine your light on, Princess, at school, at home, at church. When you walk down the street with your head held high and tiara gleaming brightly, dare to be God's girl. Not for your own glory, but to point to the beauty and love of your Father, the King.

If you see your sister's light going dim, don't be harsh and preachy. Shine your own light of love fully on her, and see if you can help her discover what's taking the glow out of her star. Encourage her to be the light God created her to be, as you shine steadily on her, not giving up 'til she's shining once again.

Journal Questions

1. Jesus said that when you see Him, you see the Father (see John 14:9). In what ways can people see Jesus when they look at you?

_____

_____

_____

_____

_____

_____

2. Jesus said to let your light shine so that others can see your good works (see Matthew 5:16). Are those good works done with your own power? Or does God enable you to do the good works?

_____

_____

_____

_____

_____

3. If you are not letting your light shine, how does that affect the people around you?

_____

_____

_____

_____

_____

_____

4. What are some things you can do to shine your light even more?

_____

_____

_____

_____

_____

5. Think of a sister who is going through a rough time and needs encouragement. List some ways you can lighten her load, and pray for strength to help her.

_____

_____

_____

_____

_____

_____

You, O Lord, keep my lamp burning; my God turns my darkness into light.

Psalm 18:28 NIV

Don't become partners with
those who reject God. How can
you make a partnership out
of right and wrong?
That's not partnership; that's war.

—*2 Corinthians 6:14 MSG*

Don't Date the Devil—No Matter How Fine He Is

Not everything that looks good is.

Isaiah 14 tells the story of an angel who was once close to God. But he grew jealous of God and thought to himself, *"I will ascend into heaven, I will exalt my throne above the stars of God"* (Isaiah 14:13 NKJV). He didn't stop there. He decided, *"I will be like the Most High"* (verse 14 NKJV).

But when Satan tried to exalt himself, the Almighty brought him down: *"Instead of climbing up you came down—down with the underground dead, down to the abyss of the Pit"* (verse 15 MSG).

The Word of God says that Satan transforms himself into an angel of light. It stands to reason that his children can do the same. Maybe the fine young man with the dazzling smile and gorgeous eyes can sing like an angel. Maybe he can even quote you scriptures. He may even go to church. But that doesn't mean he belongs to God. And if he doesn't belong to God, he cannot belong to you.

DEALING WITH A PRINCE

It doesn't matter what other girls do. Your standard is a high one. *"Those who belong to Christ Jesus have nailed the passions and desires of their sinful natures to his cross"* (Galatians 5:24 NLT). God knows that you may feel lonely at times. He understands that you may wonder if a prince will ever come for you. But, Princess, you must trust your heavenly Father. He will give you all good things in His time. Wait for Him. And stay clear of the enemy.

You can live a pure life. How? Scripture asks and answers the same question*: "How can a young [woman] live a pure life? By obeying your word"* (Psalm 119:9 NCV).

When you are tempted, ask yourself some hard questions: *"Is light best friends with dark? Does Christ go strolling with the Devil? Do trust and mistrust hold hands?"* (2 Corinthians 6:15 MSG). God has said this to you: *"Don't link up with those who pollute you. I want you all to myself. I'll be a Father to you; and you'll be [daughters] to me" (verse 18).* God wants you to Himself—not to keep you from having a social life, but to protect you from harm and preserve your most precious gifts for a prince who is worthy of you. Father really does know best.

Don't date the Devil, Princess—no matter how fine he is.

Always Sisters SISTER TIP

If your sister gets tangled up with a devil, don't just stand by and watch it happen. Don't be afraid to remind her of who she is! And help her see who he is! The Devil can dress up in a pretty fine-looking exterior. It's up to you to help your sister see past the pretty face and into his heart.

Journal Questions

1. Why is it a bad idea to date a young man who doesn't know Christ?

_____

_____

_____

_____

_____

_____

_____

_____

2. How can you tell if a young man is a Prince—a member of God's Royal Family, or not?

_____

_____

_____

_____

_____

3. Read Psalm 68:6. Loneliness is a real issue, but guys are not the only remedy. This psalm says we can rely on our families to help us not be lonely. How can you rely on your physical family to overcome loneliness? Your church family?

_____

_____

_____

_____

_____

4. What are the benefits of *waiting* rather than *dating*—even if the guy you are interested in is a Christian?

_____

_____

_____

_____

_____

5. Write a prayer asking God to bring you a godly man at just the right time. Ask for help in trusting God's plan for you and for help in knowing which man is the one God intends for you.

_____

_____

_____

_____

_____

_____

Become wise by walking with the wise; hang out with fools and watch your life fall to pieces.

Proverbs 13:20 MSG

My little children, for whom I
labor in birth again, until Christ
is formed in you, I would like to be
present with you now.

—*Galatians 4:19–20 NKJV*

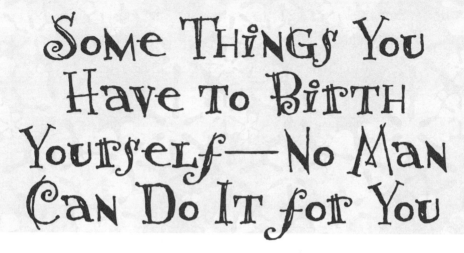

Some Things You Have to Birth Yourself—No Man Can Do It for You

In Paul's letter to the believers in Galatians, he called them "little children." They struggled to grow spiritually and repeatedly fell into error. But the apostle loved them, not only as a spiritual father can, but also with the tenderness of a spiritual mother. He spoke of the pain he experienced watching them stumble in sin as being like the labor pains a pregnant woman experiences in childbirth.

Jesus's mother had to birth Him. And because He was conceived of the Holy Spirit when she was a virgin, she accepted Him with faith. When the angel Gabriel announced that she'd been chosen to bear God's Son, she said, *"I am willing to be used of the Lord. Let it happen to me as you have said"* (Luke 1:38 NLV).

The Holy Spirit has gifts for all of God's princesses, but you have to receive them with faith, just as Mary did. You will carry those gifts inside you. But make no mistake, like the apostle Paul, you will labor to bring those spiritual gifts into the world.

Giving birth *hurts*! And it doesn't happen instantly. It can take hours—even days. Labor is work—the kind you do alone. In this life, you will labor to grow into the woman God wants you to be. Sometimes it will be hard labor.

Many princesses eagerly await their prince's arrival, believing that he will save them. They believe that just like in fairy tales, he will find them sleeping or locked away in a tower, and with one kiss he will awaken them, defeat the evil one on their behalf, and carry them away to happily ever after.

Princess, no one but God will save you.

A prince can't shape or make you either. A young man may *see* your beauty, but he won't *make* you beautiful. He can recognize your intelligence, but he won't shape your intelligence. There are gifts that come only from God and the hard work *you* do to become a young woman pleasing in God's sight. There are lessons you learn only from following your heavenly Father into hard places and narrow roads.

Some things you have to birth yourself—no man can do it for you. But God will equip you for the task. When the time comes, will you say, "Yes, I see it all now," as Mary did? If you do, Princess, even the angels will say of you:

"You're beautiful with God's beauty,
Beautiful inside and out!
God be with you." (Luke 1:28 MSG)

Always Sisters SISTER TIP

If you see your sister looking to a man for her value and worth, remind her that although a man (or boy) can see her worth, he cannot create it—and she is most definitely not dependent on him for it. It is God who has created in her the gifts worth valuing, and she is the one who develops those gifts.

Journal Questions

1. Read Galatians 4:19. What do you think Paul meant when he said to the Galatian believers that he labored in birth again, until Christ be formed in them?

_____

_____

_____

_____

_____

_____

_____

2. What kinds of spiritual gifts has God put inside you that need to be birthed spiritually?

_____

_____

_____

_____

_____

3. What do you think it means to labor (work hard) to become the woman God wants you to be? What will that work look like?

_____

_____

_____

_____

_____

_____

4. What is the role of a prince in the life of a princess (since his role is *not* to shape and make you)?

_____

_____

_____

_____

_____

5. Write a prayer asking God to birth your spiritual gifts (be specific). Praise Him for making your worth dependent on Him rather than on men or earthly things.

_____

_____

_____

_____

_____

_____

God is the one who began this good work in you, and I am certain that He won't stop before it is complete on the day that Christ Jesus returns.

Philippians 1:6 CEV

You can't say that our bodies were
made for sexual immorality.
They were made for the Lord,
and the Lord cares
about our bodies.

—*1 Corinthians 6:13 NLT*

Value Your Virtue

PRINCESS, YOU HAVE power. We're not just talking about the kind of power that allows you to run for president or be the head of a corporation. We're talking about a secret, intimate power—the power of your femininity.

You are wonderfully made and different from a man. Thank God! That's what makes you attractive to men. Women are soft, round, and lovely to captivate the attention of males. You are different by design.

Your attraction is not merely your physical beauty. You are also *spiritually* soft and receptive to a man's needs. A true prince will recognize you as someone created by God to see into his heart. You are equipped to understand him in ways he has always longed to be known. God said, "It is not good for man to be alone." You are God's gift so that man would not have to be alone—you are God's precious gift.

Princess, know that you are a unique blend of mystery, creativity, grace, and allure. There are gifts and treasure and untold beauty within you, but these treasures are meant to be shared only with your Prince—the man you will marry. The Song of Solomon says this about your precious gifts: *You are like a private garden, my treasure, my bride! You are a spring that no one else can drink from, a fountain of my own.* (Song of Solomon 4:12 NLT)

Solomon described his beloved's secret place as a garden, a spring, a fountain, using words that speak of nourishment and refreshment. And look what he said about his "spring": *no one else can drink from* it. This refers to her virginity. It is a treasure she will share only with him.

The world will see no value in your garden. If you fling open your gates carelessly, you can be sure that men will trample over your delights. *"God did not call us to be impure, but to live a holy life"* (1 Thessalonians 4:7 NIV).

If you are a princess who has already opened her garden before its time, be assured that a new beginning can be yours. When the woman of many men washed Jesus's dusty feet with her sorrowful tears, He lifted her head and looked into her eyes (see Luke 7:36–50). Yes, He told her in no uncertain terms: "No more sinning; no more messing around!" But He also offered tender words of hope and a future when He said, *"Go!"* He was saying, walk into your new life as a free woman, forgiven and clean. (More on this great story in chapter 19.)

If a young man is not willing to treat you with the respect that Jesus Himself would, he is not worthy of you. You belong to Christ first. Wait for the mate who looks like Him.

Value your virtue, Princess. God does.

Let your sister know how valuable her virtue is by how respectfully you treat her. If she seems to be caught up in a competition with other girls, dressing "hot" and wishing guys would look at her, remind her that she is worth more than temporary attention from guys who don't plan to respect her. Encourage her to live pure in God's eyes.

Journal Questions

1. Why is it important to protect your secret garden?

_____

_____

_____

_____

_____

_____

_____

_____

_____

2. What are some consequences of not protecting the treasures of your garden?

_____

_____

_____

_____

_____

3. Read 1 Corinthians 6:18–20. What is it about sexual sin that is different from all other sins? How does this make you feel about protecting your virtue?

_____

_____

_____

_____

_____

4. What are some things a young man could do to honor and respect you as a princess and woman of God?

_____

_____

_____

_____

_____

5. List some ways you can encourage people to treat you with respect without being disrespectful in the process. Pray that God will show you how to do this.

_____

_____

_____

_____

_____

_____

_____

Create in me a pure heart,

O God, and renew a steadfast

spirit within me.

Psalm 51:10 NIV

I want you to know that the head of
every man is Christ,
the head of woman is man,
and the head of Christ is God.

—*1 Corinthians 11:3 NKJV*

Got You Covered

FROM THE BEGINNING God had a divine plan for His family. He created a beautiful world and a beautiful young man to inhabit it. The story is told in Genesis 2: *"And the Lord God said, 'It is not good that man should be alone; I will make him a helper comparable to him'"* (verse 18 NKJV). Notice God didn't say He'd make him a helper *inferior* to him. You are not an afterthought in God's mind.

The first thing God did was put man to sleep (see verse 21). Then he took a bone from his rib: *"Then the rib which the Lord God had taken from man He made into a woman"* (verse 22). God took a rib from the man's side, perhaps to encourage the man to *walk beside* the woman and keep her near to his heart. Adam proclaimed: *"This is now bone of my bones and flesh of my flesh"* (verse 23). Man and woman were one.

What we see in the Garden of Eden is God's ideal family. God was head of man. Man was head of woman, and all would work in their specially designed roles. Being the head simply meant a certain kind of authority.

Unfortunately, things got out of order in the Garden. The serpent came and tempted the woman. She stepped out of her role and acted as head of the man. Man stepped out of his role and obeyed the woman. And everything went down from there (see Genesis 3).

Things still go wrong when you step out of your rightful, God-ordained role. Princess, one day your prince will come. If you and your husband-prince live by God's design, he will be the head of your family and will cover you, keeping you from harm and the snares of the enemy that entrapped Eve in the Garden of Eden. And God will cover him with His protection.

Following God's plan, your husband's head will be Christ. He will submit to Christ in love and service. And Christ, dear Princess, submits to God, but not because He is inferior to God, for He is God, and Christ and God are equally divine. Rather, Christ submits to God because this is His God-ordained role. Princess, you and your prince are also equal beings, but you have different roles.

God's got you covered. Trust His design.

Always **SISTERS** SISTER TIP

Make a pact with your sister to watch out for the kinds of boys and men you allow into your lives. Encourage each other to hang around only with the kind of men who treat you with the honor and protection that God intended—the kind of men you can one day look up to as head of your family. When those handsome "devils" come calling, keep your sister's eyes and heart on the kind of man who will cover her with love and dignity.

JOURNAL QUESTIONS

1. What can happen if a young woman is not covered at all?

_____

_____

_____

_____

_____

_____

_____

2. God is the spiritual head of all families, but who is the head in your family if no father is present?

_____

_____

_____

_____

_____

3. Who covers a young woman before she is married?

_____

_____

_____

_____

_____

4. Read Ephesians 5:25–33. What are the blessings and benefits of God's plan for coverage?

_____

_____

_____

_____

_____

5. Think of someone you know who has a good marriage. List the qualities of the husband and the wife that seem to help make the marriage good.

_____

_____

_____

_____

_____

_____

Lord, you have assigned me my portion and my cup; you have made my lot secure. The boundary lines have fallen for me in pleasant places; surely I have a delightful inheritance. . . . You have made known to me the path of life; you will fill me with joy in your presence, with eternal pleasures at your right hand.

Psalm 16:5–11 NIV

Exercise daily in God—
no spiritual flabbiness, please!
Workouts in the gymnasium are
useful, but a disciplined life in God
is far more so, making you fit
both today and forever.

—*I Timothy 4:8 MSG*

Which Two B's— Breast and Behind or Bible and Brains?

She has it going on. She spends hours at the gym, working her body to perfection. When she walks down the hallway at school, all eyes are on her. Her shirt, clinging to her breasts, is cut so low you can almost see her belly button. Her nearly painted-on jeans and high-heeled shoes show off her sculpted legs. She leaves nothing to the imagination; every contour of her body is accentuated. Boys swarm around her like flies, and even some of the girls envy the attention she commands.

She doesn't study. She doesn't think she has to. She thinks she'll get by on her looks alone. She uses her body like currency, spending it wildly with no thought of saving something for tomorrow.

But maybe beneath all the provocative clothes is a scared little girl who has no idea that she's meant to be a princess. Perhaps she feels she has nothing but her body to contribute to the world. Maybe she feels vulnerable. If you look at the outer shell, you won't see the soft center that can be so easily hurt. Her physical form, which she tones and primes to perfection, takes the attention off her flabby and malnourished soul.

Princess, don't be like her, putting more emphasis on working out your body instead of working out your salvation in fear and trembling (see Philippians 2:12). That's not to say you shouldn't take care of your body. Paul said, "*Workouts in the gymnasium are useful*" (1 Timothy 4:8 MSG)—that is, if you want to build your natural body. But Paul goes on to say that "*a disciplined life in God is far more so, making you fit both today and forever.*" Rather than focusing only on the *b and b* of breast and behind, choose instead to add spiritual strength through your Bible and brains *b and b*.

Hear these words spoken just to you as a young woman of God: "*Let no one despise your youth, but be an example to the believers in word, in conduct, in love, in spirit, in faith, in purity. . . . Give attention to reading, to exhortation, to doctrine. Do not neglect the gift that is in you*" (1 Timothy 4:11–14 NKJV).

How can you do that? Prayer, studying, and meditating on God's Word are powerful ways to build up your spirit. Fasting is a spiritual discipline that packs a punch. Praising God and spending time alone in His presence—all these things keep you in beautiful shape for eternity, fit and fine for the Kingdom of God.

Working out with your sister can be fun. How about setting up a time to "work out" together spiritually? Make specific plans, like, "Let's get together Monday after school and share our favorite scripture for the week and pray about what's going on in our lives." Keep it real, and keep your appointment.

Journal Questions

1. Is it wrong to put time into taking care of your body? How can you build a proper balance between taking care of your body and taking care of your soul?

_____

_____

_____

_____

_____

_____

_____

DEALING WITH A PRINCE

2. Read 1 Timothy 4:8. Why is a disciplined life in God more useful than workouts at the gymnasium?

_____

_____

_____

_____

_____

3. This devotional is about building Bible and brains. How do spiritual disciplines build brains?

_____

_____

_____

_____

_____

_____

4. What spiritual disciplines do you practice now? What can you add? Write down the time and place you will begin.

_____

_____

_____

_____

_____

_____

5. Write down specific plans to include your sister in a spiritual workout, and pray for those plans to succeed.

_____

_____

_____

_____

_____

_____

_____

His divine power has given us everything we need for life and godliness through our knowledge of him who called us by his own glory and goodness.

2 Peter 1:3 NIV

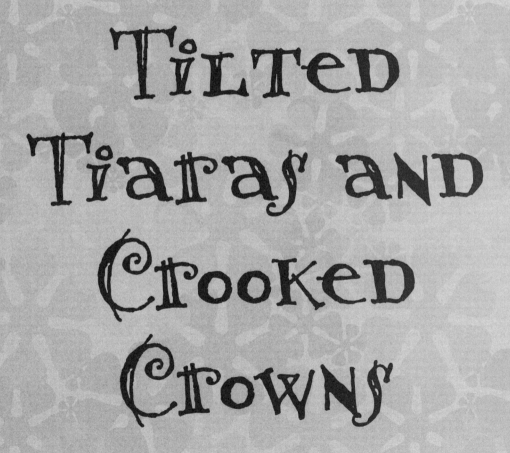

Tilted Tiaras and Crooked Crowns

I will give you rest

Jesus said, "Come to me, all of you who are weary and carry heavy burdens, and I will give you rest."

—*Matthew 11:28 NLT*

Not for Perfect Princesses— Dealing with Your Stuff

SISTERS ARE SISTERS, no matter what. But if you're like most of the sisters out there—you have been through some *stuff*.

Now, when you tell yourself the truth, you might have to admit that some of the stuff you did to yourself. Like some bad choices you've made. You know; maybe you didn't behave like the princess God created you to be when you were out with that fine brother the other night. Or maybe you disrespected your mother or your teacher and got into some pretty serious trouble. The truth is, the kind of *stuff* we're talking about is really something nobody likes to talk about: *sin*—and you, Princess, have to deal with it.

There's also a good chance that there's been some foul stuff done *to* you that you had no control over—where somebody sinned against *you*. This is stuff that you aren't responsible for, but it leaves you feeling heavy and crushed. Stuff that's got your heart burdened and your head low—like you don't have the right to look up at the sun or into the faces of the people passing by.

But, guess what, Sister! Your Father God—who is a good, good, Father—already knows your stuff, all of it! He has His big, gentle finger under your chin, and He's tenderly lifting your chin and sayin' so soft, "Look up, Baby Girl, look up. You're *my* child. You're a daughter of the King. You're my little princess."

And He points your face toward the face of His Son—because in that face, you'll find forgiveness for the stuff you did to yourself and you'll find the strength to overcome the stuff others did to you.

Hebrews 4:15–16 (TEV) says, *"Our High Priest is not one who cannot feel sympathy for our weaknesses. . . . Let us . . . approach God's throne where there is grace. There we will receive mercy and find grace to help us just when we need it."* The thing about being God's princess is that He knows you've got stuff in your life; He knows you stumble sometimes and tilt your tiara. But He's there to straighten your crooked crown and give you a fresh, new robe of righteousness because He loves you.

The Bible also teaches us how to deal with the stuff that other people have done to us. Ephesians 4:32 (TLB) tells us: *"Be kind to one another, tender-hearted, forgiving one another, just as God has forgiven you because you belong to Christ."* As a princess, forgiveness is part of your heritage. You have forgiveness through Christ, and through Him, you can forgive.

You're a daughter of the King—bring Him your stuff and see what wonderful things He will do in your life.

Always Sisters SISTER TIP

Watch out for your sister. If you see that she's down and hurting, ask her why. Be someone she can share her stuff with. Help her figure out which things she can do something about and which things are totally out of her control. Just asking and listening can go a long way toward healing.

Journal Questions

1. It can be scary to tell the truth about ourselves—even to ourselves. But, here, in the privacy of this book, dare to put words to the *stuff* that's been stuffed inside you for way too long. Let's start with the stuff you have done to yourself. Read Psalm 38:18 and 1 John 1:9. Now, take a chance. Put words to your feelings, and write them down.

———————————————————————————

———————————————————————————

———————————————————————————

———————————————————————————

_____

_____

_____

_____

2. Some of the pain we feel has been caused by what others have done to us. List here what was done to you that was totally out of your control.

_____

_____

_____

_____

_____

_____

_____

_____

_____

When you're done with your list, write across it, "Not Guilty!" Though this stuff was done to you, it was not your fault. The burden of guilt is not yours! Let it go.

3. Though forgiveness is not easy, it is _freedom_! Holding grudges against those who have caused you pain hurts you, not them. Write a prayer asking God to soften your heart so that you can forgive. I'll get you started:

Father, some of the people in my life have hurt me real bad. They've taken advantage of me, used me, and made me feel I wasn't worth anything. Soften my heart so that I can let go of the pain I feel and begin to forgive . . .

_____

_____

_____

_____

_____

_____

_____

Instead of their shame my people
will receive a double portion
and instead of disgrace they will
rejoice in their inheritance;
. . . For I the LORD love justice. . . .
All who see them will
acknowledge that they are a
people the LORD has blessed.
Isaiah 61:7–9 NIV

I forgive your sins

Then [Jesus] spoke to her:
"I forgive your sins."

—*Luke 7:48 MSG*

X-Girls—God Forgives What You Leave Behind

Every girl is an X-girl. And some girls have very bad X's. You may be an X-overeater or an X-constant complainer. Maybe you're an X-doubter. But some girls are X-prostitutes. Or X-exotic dancers. Some have X's even worse than those.

Jesus didn't seem to mind X-girls. He talked to them all the time. There was one very bad X-girl he talked to at a dinner party when no one else there would.

One of the Pharisees asked [Jesus] over for a meal. He went to the Pharisee's house and sat down at the dinner table. Just then a woman of the village, the town harlot, having learned that Jesus was a guest in the home of the Pharisee, came with a bottle of very expensive perfume and stood at his feet, weeping, raining tears on his feet. Letting down her hair she dried his feet, kissed them, and anointed them with the perfume. (Luke 7:36–38 MSG)

The other men in the room, some of them religious teachers, couldn't stand the sinful X-girl. One of them, Simon, thought less of her than anyone else present. He said to himself, *"If this man was the prophet I thought he was, he would have known what kind of woman this is who is falling all over him"* (Luke 7:39).

Jesus called the man to himself: *"Simon, I have something to tell you."*

Then Jesus told a story.

Two men were in debt to a banker. One owed five hundred silver pieces, the other fifty. Neither of them could pay up, and so the banker canceled both debts. Which of the two would be more grateful?

Simon answered, "I suppose the one who was forgiven the most."

"That's right," said Jesus. Then turning to the woman, but speaking to Simon, he said, "Do you see this woman? I came into your home; you provided no water for my feet, but she rained tears on my feet and dried them with her hair. You gave me no greeting, but from the time I arrived she hasn't quit kissing my feet. You provided nothing for freshening up, but she has soothed my feet with perfume. Impressive, isn't it? She was forgiven many, many sins, and so she is very, very grateful. If the forgiveness is minimal, the gratitude is minimal."

Then he spoke to her: "I forgive your sins." (Luke 7:40–48)

It doesn't matter how many X's you have, Princess. Jesus has lifted your hung-down head, looked deeply into your tear-filled eyes, and said, "I forgive your sins." He doesn't keep score. He doesn't even *remember* your sins.

That woman with her bottle of fragrant gratitude walked out of that house *saved.* Jesus said, *"Your faith has saved you. Go in peace"* (verse 50). No matter what life or sins or X's you leave behind, Princess, you are forgiven. Jesus says to you the same: You are saved. Go in peace.

Be to your sister what Jesus was to the woman in this story: a forgiving friend. Be the kind of friend she can share her past sins with; then remind her not only of God's forgiveness but also of His command to sin no more and go in peace.

Journal Questions

1. The people in the woman's village did not approve of her and probably never would. If some people don't believe in you, how does God's love and belief in you help you to begin again?

   _____

   _____

   _____

   _____

   _____

   _____

2. The story says the woman rained tears on Jesus's feet. How important is it to feel truly sorry for your sins?

_____

_____

_____

_____

_____

3. Jesus told the woman her faith had saved her and to go in peace. How do you think He intended for her to live the rest of her life?

_____

_____

_____

_____

_____

4. Read Ephesians 1:7–8. Knowing in your head that you're forgiven and accepting it in your heart are two different things. But eventually the truth of God's Word will make its way to your heart. Read the verses above again, and write what they mean to you.

_____

_____

_____

_____

_____

5. How can you have peace when you've done so many wrong things?

_____

_____

_____

_____

_____

_____

_____

There is now no condemnation for those who are in Christ Jesus.

Romans 8:1 NIV

I will never leave you

For He himself has said,
"I will never leave you
nor forsake you."

—*Hebrews 13:5 NKJV*

WHEN EVERYONE ELSE WALKS AWAY, GOD STAYS

"I WILL NEVER leave you nor forsake you." Few other promises in God's Word are as absolute as this. It's as if the writer of the book of Hebrews wants to make double sure that we get the message, because he uses two phrases that mean almost the same thing: "I'll never leave you; I'll never forsake you." Isn't it wonderful to think that God makes the effort to let you know how much He cares for you? It makes God's tenderness, not just as Father but as Abba—Daddy—so much more real.

Not only will Jesus never leave you. He won't change His mind about it. Look what God says about Jesus your King in the very first chapter of Hebrews:

> You're God, and on the throne for good;
>> your rule makes everything right.
> You love it when things are right;
>> you hate it when things are wrong.
> That is why God, your God,
>> poured fragrant oil on your head,

117

Marking you out as king,

Far above your dear companions. (Hebrews 1:8–9 MSG)

And:

You, Master, started it all, laid earth's foundations,

then crafted the stars in the sky.

Earth and sky will wear out, but not you;

they become threadbare like an old coat;

You'll fold them up like a worn-out cloak,

and lay them away on the shelf.

But you'll stay the same, year after year;

you'll never fade, you'll never wear out. (Hebrews 1:10 MSG)

Princess, you belong to a King who is everlasting. He is unchanging. The One who flung the bright, white stars into the inky night will not fade to black or dissolve into nothingness. He'll outlast the earth and the sky. And in all that timelessness, He will remember you, have mercy on you, and be with you.

In the course of a well-lived life, you will meet many people. Friends will change as you change—in your mind, your heart, even your geography. Faces will come with places, and then they will go. You will win loves and lose them. Eventually you will say good-bye to everyone you've ever loved, or they will say good-bye to you—at least in this life.

But no matter who walks away, no matter why he or she departs, Jesus will stay. He'll never, ever, ever go away.

Believe it.

Your sister may have someone in her life who has left her—maybe someone who promised he or she would never leave, but the promise was broken. Recite Hebrews 13:5 to her: "For He Himself has said, 'I will never leave you nor forsake you'" (NKJV). Then help her to lift her eyes off the pain in this world and look to the One who never walks away.

Journal Questions

1. Read Hebrews 13:5 again. Why do you think God used two phrases that mean almost the same thing: *"never leave you"* and *"never forsake you"*?

_____

_____

_____

_____

_____

_____

_____

2. When God says He will never leave you, does He mean that you can sin as much as you want?

_____

_____

_____

_____

_____

3. If you continue to sin, will God change His mind and leave you? Or would your own actions mean that it's *you* who doesn't want to be with Him?

_____

_____

_____

_____

_____

_____

4. Jesus is King of creation. That is awesome power. How does it make you feel to know that God Himself loves you enough to never let you go?

_____

_____

_____

_____

_____

_____

5. Give an example of when God was there for you when everyone else walked away.

_____

_____

_____

_____

_____

_____

_____

Because of the Lord's great love

we are not consumed,

for his compassions never fail.

They are new every morning;

great is your faithfulness.

Lamentations 3:22-23 NIV

Seventy times seven

At that point Peter got up the nerve
to ask, "Master, how many times do
I forgive a brother or sister who
hurts me? Seven?"
Jesus replied, "Seven! Hardly!
Try seventy times seven."

—*Matthew 18:21–22 MSG*

Forgiving Yourself and Those Who Have Mistreated You

JESUS LOVES A good story. He told them all the time. When Peter asked Him about forgiveness, part of Jesus's answer was a story (see Matthew 18:23–35). He told Peter that the Kingdom of Heaven was like a king who wanted to get money matters straight with some of his servants. He began to work on settling his accounts, and a servant was brought to him who owed him an enormous amount of money. In the New King James Version, it says he owed the king ten thousand talents.

The poor man couldn't begin to pay so much money back. His master commanded that he, his wife, his children, and everything that he had be sold to pay his debt. The servant begged for mercy, and the compassionate king forgave his debt—every bit of it.

Later that day, the same man whose debt had been forgiven found someone who owed *him* money—one hundred denarii. He must have forgotten the compassion the king showed him because he took his debtor by the throat and demanded that he pay what he owed. He didn't budge when the man begged for mercy, even though he had just received mercy from the king. Rather, he threw the man into jail, forgiving him nothing. Others witnessed his cruelty and reported back to the king. The king was not happy. He said, *"You wicked servant! I forgave you all that debt because you begged me. Should you not also have had compassion on your fellow servant, just as I had pity on you?"* (Matthew 18:32–33 NKJV). Sadly, the story doesn't have a good ending: that wicked servant was taken away to be tortured.

In the time of Jesus, a denarius was worth an entire day's wages. In today's dollar (which is constantly changing in worth), a denarius would be worth approximately $50. One talent was *six thousand* denarii or $300,000! Imagine ten thousand times $300,000. That would make $3 billion! The servant was forgiven $3 billion but wouldn't forgive another's debt of one hundred days' wages, or $5,000.

We've all sinned. Even the best princesses owe God far more than they can possibly pay back. Jesus, the compassionate King, gives His mercy. He wipes debt out with His own blood. Completely!

Doesn't it stand to reason that you should be quick to forgive? Seven times a day? Hardly! Seventy times seven was Jesus's way of saying that you can't count how many times to forgive. Just forgive, as often as you have to—no matter who has hurt you, no matter how badly, even if the person you must forgive is *you*.

Your King, Jesus, has forgiven all. Princess, you must do the same. He'll help you with it. Remember, He's the one who'll never leave you. The power to forgive will come from Him. Borrow His compassion, and spend it all!

To keep your "always sister" relationships strong, don't hold on to grudges or hang on to anger. If your sister wrongs you, either let it go, or talk it through—but don't hold it against her. Forgive as you have been forgiven.

Journal Questions

1. Have you ever behaved like the unforgiving servant? When has it been hard for you to forgive?

_____

_____

_____

_____

_____

_____

_____

2. Read Luke 6:34–36. Does someone owe you a debt—something you must forgive this person for? What if he or she cannot make it up to you?

_____

_____

_____

_____

_____

3. In the story, the king delivered the unforgiving servant to the torturers until he could pay all that was due to the king. What do you think Jesus was saying in this part of the story about the fate of those who refuse to forgive?

_____

_____

_____

_____

_____

4. Have you ever forgiven a person who's done something terrible to you? How did it feel to forgive?

_____

_____

_____

_____

_____

5. Write a prayer about forgiveness—either asking God to forgive you or to help you forgive someone else.

_____

_____

_____

_____

_____

_____

_____

As God's chosen people, holy and dearly loved, clothe yourselves with compassion, kindness, humility, gentleness and patience. Bear with each other and forgive whatever grievances you may have against one another. Forgive as the Lord forgave you. And over all these virtues put on love, which binds them all together in perfect unity.

Colossians 3:12-14 NIV

Love will cover

Above all things have fervent love
for one another, for "love
will cover a multitude of sins."

—1 Peter 4:8 NKJV

Always Sisters— Covering Each Other

Who among us doesn't need the protective cover of those who love us?

God is the most powerful and precious cover of all. The prophet Isaiah calls Him our "rear guard"—the one who brings up the end of the war party and protects those ahead of Him: *"God is leading you out of here, and the Lord God of Israel is also your rear guard"* (Isaiah 52:12 MSG).

Yes, God is your chief rear guard—but He will often cover you through the women circled around you. Sometimes that cover begins with a mother's prayer. Her prayers become wings for her wayward daughter to fly free from the trouble she's gotten herself into—stuff she shouldn't have even been thinking about. Or maybe a mother will cover her girl in prayer over hurtful things that girl couldn't have anticipated—some unthinkable horror that visited her through no fault of her own. But Mother prayed, Jesus heard, and He called her baby out.

At other times, that cover comes from a loving sister-friend, who sees you leaving your terror and following Jesus. You follow Him wholeheartedly, without asking any questions, clutching your tiny mustard seed of faith. But you're vulnerable. You need a rear guard. That's when your sisters come in. Protecting you. Loving you. Asking for nothing in return but that you keep following Jesus, come what may.

Princess, you need the love of your sisters in this world. They won't let you be ashamed. You are sisters in the struggle, no matter whether you've had the same experiences or not. You share so much in sisterhood simply because you are women who belong to God.

Look closely at the words of the song:

Always sisters, always friends,

Let's stay real close 'til the end

Forgiving each other, letting love cover

Always sisters, always friends.

Carry the words in your heart. Embrace your sisters, love them fiercely. And when one is naked and ashamed, cover her. Be a sister. Always be ready to hand over your own coat to keep someone else warm. Be fearless. God will protect you.

He'll send a rear guard to cover you too.

No matter what may come or go

We stick together and it shows.

This bond between us foundation is trust

That's what true family is all about.

When you see your sister in trouble, come up beside her and be her cover. Remember the encouragement in 1 Peter 4:8: "Above all things have fervent love for one another, for 'love will cover a multitude of sins'" (NKJV). Every sister is broken and hurting in some places. Your unconditional sisterly love has the power to heal and to cover. Forgive, encourage, and lift her up. That's what sisters are for.

Journal Questions

1. Many princesses believe they can't get along with other women. Why do you think this is?

_____

_____

_____

_____

_____

_____

2. In what ways can you show fervent love for your sisters—the kind of love that "*covers a multitude of sins*" (1 Peter 4:8 NKJV)?

_____

_____

_____

_____

_____

3. What if you find a sister has gotten herself in a terrible predicament, and it's all her fault? How could you encourage her?

_____

_____

_____

_____

_____

4. Read Galatians 6:2. How are you your sister's keeper? List some ways you *have* carried or *could* carry her burdens.

_____

_____

_____

_____

_____

5. Write a prayer of blessing for those sisters in your life who stand behind you as part of God's rear guard, and ask God to show you how to guard the sister next to you.

_____

_____

_____

_____

_____

_____

_____

So let's do it—full of belief, confident that we're presentable inside and out. Let's keep a firm grip on the promises that keep us going. He always keeps his word. Let's see how inventive we can be in encouraging love and helping out.

Hebrews 10:23-25 MSG

AUTHOR CHAT

1. *What inspired your interest in mentoring young women?*

   Ever since I was seventeen, young women have written me, telling me about their problems and asking my advice, and it has made me realize that young women need mentors who can provide a good foundation and encouragement to be all they can be.

2. *What do you see as the main challenge girls face?*

   When you look at all the things girls go through, most of their problems stem from not seeing themselves as God sees them. Girls today face difficult situations, and having to face them with a false view of themselves—not knowing their value in God's eyes—is their main challenge.

3. *What advice do you wish someone had told you when you were younger?*

   I have been blessed to have always had godly people speak into my life, so I had a strong sense of faith and who I was, even when I was very young. But what I missed was having more encouragement to realize that as women we have power to accomplish whatever we want to accomplish, not just at home but in whatever career we choose.

4. *Have the "always sisters" in your life held you up or held you accountable?*

   My "always sisters"—my natural sisters, as well as my friend sisters—have held me up; they intercede for me, they are a safe place for me, and I know they love me and are always praying for me. They are fun and keep me laughing, but they also hold me accountable, and they definitely tell it like it is and will let me know if I'm straying away from the truth. They are giants in my life.

5. *Have you ever struggled with self-esteem issues?*

   I have, and still do, even to this day. Low self-esteem is a recurring problem in the lives of women—it's like dealing with the enemy within yourself. Your battles may be different, but while you're fighting them you always have to remind yourself of your worth in Jesus so you don't lose sight of who you are. The Bible says to take up your cross daily and to study to show yourself approved, which helps remind you who you are so you can consistently be strengthened and have your worth reiterated.

6. *What was your toughest challenge as a teenager?*

   My toughest challenge as a teenager was probably accepting the road to becoming who I am today—stepping out and singing. I cried through my first solo performance at age eight, and I cried every time I had to repeat that performance. I never liked being out front—singing in the background was perfect for me! But with practice I became comfortable with it. At sixteen I realized my voice was more than a talent; it was a calling, and it looked as if I was going to be out front for a while. I was terrified, but I listened to my calling and learned to accept the challenge.

7. *What was the most positive influence on you when you were younger?*
   By far the most positive influence on me was my mom. She's a strong, yet soft, woman. Even though she was very tender with us growing up, we knew not to mess with her! She taught us what was right, but she lived it as well. She always worked outside the home but was able to keep things running *inside* the home as well. Now that I'm older, I am amazed at how she did everything. Vocally, I was influenced by Tramaine Hawkins and Gladys Knight. I learned that singing with passion was just as important, if not more important, as vocal ability.

8. *How do you help a friend who is in trouble without being pulled down to get into trouble yourself?*
   When you see a sister struggle, you can give her good advice, love her, and pray for her, but you shouldn't follow her. For example, if you see a friend who is sad, you can easily get depressed. You have to be filled with hope in order to bring hope, so you need prayer to keep your spirit up. If your sister is involved in something wrong, don't go along with her. Even if she is a close

friend, you may have to keep your distance from her to keep from being led down the same path. You can't compromise what is right to help a friend, and you may need to bring in someone you both respect to help with the situation. Your example of prayer and love, while refusing to do wrong with her, is the best way to help her.

9. *What is your vision for young women today?*

My vision for young women today is for them to be happy, and happiness comes from knowing who they are and whose they are and from knowing their value. Finding their power, passion, and purpose will lead to their happiness. I don't want their vision to be messed up because of someone else's vision; it needs to be their own.

10. *Have you seen evidence of how your vision is spreading through your conferences?*

I've seen it, and it is so exciting—we have testimonies that are incredible, of how the girls' lives have changed and how their relationships with their moms and sisters have become richer and better. We've inspired young women and given them hope by helping them realize they are daughters of the King. What a blessing for me to see their faces with hope and excitement about being at the conferences, to know they are loved and specially made, to see them cheering on each other and getting away from competition and jealousy.

11. *What's your favorite song?*

    That is such a hard question to answer! There are so many great songs out there. But I would have to say that "You Are the Sunshine of My Life" is one of my all-time favorites. When I was younger I remember hearing it come on the radio at the local candy store. It's such a feel-good song, and it would always make me emotional: sometimes it made me smile; sometimes it made me cry. It's both a love song and a spiritual song—I feel like that's the way God feels about us.

12. *God has blessed you with a beautiful voice. Was there ever a time when you wished for a different gift?*

    I never wanted to turn in the gift I have, although I have wished for more gifts, or a better gift. But over the years when you learn to appreciate your gift, you realize that you are an important part of the puzzle, that nobody can be you, that God created you for a purpose, and that He never makes a mistake. When you get a handle on that, you nourish your gift. I admire other gifts, but I'm more than satisfied with what I've been given.

13. *One of your journal questions asks girls to tell about a time when God provided for them, even when they couldn't see how He would do it. Was there a time like that in your life, when God provided for you when you couldn't see how He would do it?*

    There have been so very many times when God provided for me. One that comes to mind was when my next to the oldest brother needed surgery and was told he would die, with or without the surgery. My family decided to go ahead with the surgery, but we called in every person of faith we knew to pray for him. During the surgery the doctor came out to tell us that my brother's heart exploded, and my father asked the surgeon if he minded if we prayed for him right then to help my brother through the surgery. The surgeon let us pray over him, and my brother made it through the surgery fine and was able to live for eight more years. The doctors couldn't explain how he made it through, but we knew it was God. Later, at my brother's homegoing, we found out that the doctor and nurses in the operating room had come to believe in Jesus because of that experience with my brother.

More About CeCe

A SIX-TIME GRAMMY winner, CeCe Winans is also the recipient of a staggering amount of Gospel Music Association and Stellar awards. *Purified* is perhaps her most personal and candid album yet, with tracks like "Always Sisters," which is the inspiration for her Always Sisters conferences. Finding the beauty of God's well of inspiration in both the sacred and the secular, CeCe Winans seamlessly segues from R&B to pop to deeply felt gospel fervor, showcasing the crystalline vocals, celestial melodies, and top-shelf musical elements that have made her one of the most popular and influential artists working in contemporary gospel music.

Born in Detroit, Michigan, CeCe Winans is the eighth of ten children in the Winans, one of gospel music's most renowned musical families. She worked with her brother BeBe in a duo called the PTL Singers until the pair began performing as "BeBe & CeCe Winans" in 1987, becoming one of the most commercially successful gospel artists ever.